SIMPLE TIPS
TO BE A HAPPIER
YOU

DEVIN C. HUGHES

A PRODUCTION OF
DEVIN C. HUGHES ENTERPRISES, LLC

Simple Tips to Be a Happier YOU
Copyright 2018 by Devin C. Hughes

ISBN: 978-1719843454

Published by
Devin C. Hughes Enterprises, LLC
August 2018

Book and cover design:
Elizabeth Beeton
B10 Mediaworx

If you think happiness matters and want to be part of creating a happier society for everyone, then join thousands of others at www.devinchughes.com.

HELPING OTHERS MAKES YOU HAPPIER

Practicing acts of kindness releases serotonin into your brain, which makes you feel happier. People who observe an act of kindness also have serotonin released in to their brain, so doing something nice not only makes you happier, it also brings happiness to anyone that happens to be watching. *The key is to sincerely want to help.* Your motivation has to be an intrinsic desire to help someone rather than being focused on what you are going to get out of it.

Caring does not have to be connected to an organized charity. Reaching out to a friend or someone at work or school also makes you happier.

Giving to others releases endorphins that provide us with a "helper's high," similar to a "runner's high." Did you know that even after the chemicals dissipate from our bodies, we still have a long-term sense of wellbeing that can last for several months?

THE MASTER HAS NO POSSESSIONS.
THE MORE HE DOES FOR OTHERS,
THE HAPPIER HE IS. THE MORE HE GIVES
TO OTHERS, THE WEALTHIER HE IS.
– LAO TZU

Have an Attitude of Gratitude

Research shows that people who express gratitude regularly are healthier, less stressed, and more successful. Gratitude gives you something positive to focus on as you tackle the challenges life throws at you.

Every morning when you wake up, think of three things that you are grateful for. They could be as simple as having running water (something one-third of the world doesn't have) or a family, or a place to live, or a job. Remind yourself every day about the good things in your life.

Practicing Random Acts of Kindness makes you happier

Practicing kindness connects us to people in ways we might not expect when we are surprised by other people's positive reactions to what we do. Helping others helps us find a sense of meaning, helps us see how fortunate we are, and improves our mood. Physically, Acts of Kindness release serotonin in our brains and in the brains of the people who witness our Acts of Kindness. Kindness makes everyone happier.

Pick one day a week to practice Random Acts of Kindness

- ★ Set a goal, such as five acts in one day.
- ★ Tape money to a vending machine for stranger to use.
- ★ Spend $5 on a friend.
- ★ Give up your cab or your seat on the bus to someone else.
- ★ Open a door for someone or hold the elevator.
- ★ Buy a friend a drink.
- ★ Bring donuts or cakes to work for a treat.
- ★ Pay the toll fee for the person in the car behind you.
- ★ Say thank you when next at the check-in at the airport.
- ★ Give the employee in a public restroom a tip if the room is clean

BUILD YOUR HAPPINESS BY SMILING MORE

Smiles are viral. When you smile, other people catch it and they spread it to more people. We instinctually mimic another person's smile to help us determine if their smile is authentic. Smiling is like our internal radar. We send out a smile and they send a smile back. We mimic that smile and automatically interpret the results. The results enable us to intuitively know whether this person is friend or foe and what kind of mood they are in. Research also has shown that by measuring the smiles of people in their yearbook photos, scientists could predict how long-lasting and fulfilling their lives would be, how they would score on measures of wellbeing, and how inspiring they would be to others.

A SMILE IS THE SHORTEST DISTANCE
BETWEEN TWO PEOPLE.
– VICTOR BORGE

Faking a smile still makes us happy. Using our smile muscles sends positive messages to the emotional centers in the brain. So by forcing our faces to smile, we can activate the areas of our brain that make us feel better. In other words, we don't just smile as a result of being happy; smiling actually makes us happier. Smiling also increases mood-enhancing hormones like endorphins, and decreases stress-inducing hormones like cortisol, so you become healthier as well as happier.

Most importantly, smiling makes you more attractive to other people. So smile. And if you can't smile, fake it until you can.

PRACTICE OPTIMISM TO BECOME HAPPIER

Optimism changes the way we look at and remember our interactions in life. We put a more positive spin on our events and activities. By changing how we see and think about future outcomes, we influence those outcomes for the better. We work harder to keep outcomes in line with our optimistic expectations.

Numerous research studies have confirmed the benefits of optimism, which include better health, longer lives, faster recovery from illness, and even healthier babies.

A rational optimist does not necessarily ignore pessimistic thoughts; they realize that they can do something about them. We call this "Falling Up" – overcoming issues in the face of adversity.

A few tips for creating optimism in your life:

Visualize your best possible self: A future in which everything has turned out the way you want. Put a coin in a jar every time you consciously replace a pessimistic thought with an optimistic thought. When the jar is full, you can use the change to buy yourself a treat. An empty jar reminds you to keep finding ways to choose optimistic thoughts.

LET US ALWAYS MEET EACH OTHER
WITH A SMILE,
FOR THE SMILE
IS THE BEGINNING OF LOVE.
– MOTHER TERESA

PRACTICE AUTONOMY

In his book *Drive*, Daniel Pink discusses the benefits of autonomy and choosing our lives. He summarizes, "Human beings have an innate inner drive to be autonomous, self-determined, and connected to one another" and that "people oriented toward autonomy and intrinsic motivation have higher self-esteem, better interpersonal relationships, and greater general wellbeing . . . "

Research has shown autonomy results in more persistence at a task, which leads to higher grades, higher levels of productivity, and less burnout. Focus on your autonomy – what you can do versus what you can't do.

Build an autonomy list

What things in your life do you get to choose?

- ★ people with whom you spend time
- ★ activities
- ★ how you do things
- ★ what you eat
- ★ what you wear

On a regular basis, add to the list. When you find yourself frustrated or stuck, think through your choices. It's your life. You choose.

AUTONOMY LEADS TO EMPOWERMENT.
WE WORK HARD TO MAINTAIN A BALANCE
BETWEEN COLLABORATION AND
COOPERATION AND INDEPENDENCE.
– BOBBY KOTICK

SPEND TIME
IN THE SUN

Sunlight makes you happier and healthier.

Getting more sunlight is another way to be happier and healthier. Reduced exposure to sunlight can result in a form of depression called Seasonal Affective Disorder, or SAD.

SAD affects people who live in regions that are not exposed to sun for long periods of time, and their level of happiness varies with the seasons. They feel great in the spring and summer months and then get depressed in autumn and winter when they have less exposure to the sun. Sunlight is one of the highest providers of vitamin D, which is associated with an improved immune system, bone growth, and general health.

Vitamin D has been shown to decrease the risk of colon, skin, and breast cancer by as much as 60%. Sunlight is also believed to help in the production of endorphins, which also help us feel happier.

Find ways to spend time outside. Take a walk or eat your lunch outside. It will energize you and help you be healthier and happier.

THE SIX BEST DOCTORS:
SUNSHINE – WATER – REST
AIR – EXERCISE – DIET.
– WAYNE FIELDS

GIVE A FEW HUGS EACH DAY

Build happier relationships with hugs.

In our personal relationships, hugs help us feel closer, build trust, and improve communication with the other person.

Hugs have also been shown to improve memory, reduce stress, and provide a feeling of safety. This is not just an emotional reaction; it is also a physical one. Hugs release oxytocin, a "relationship hormone." It is found in increased levels between mothers and their newborn babies, and in people with positive romantic relationships. Hugging also increases serotonin levels, which helps us feel happier and more relaxed. Hugs help improve the immune system and the production of white blood cells and help us release tension.

Hugs are another way of communicating the importance of people in our lives. Hugging sends the message that they are important to us and they matter. Hugs open us up when we are feeling constrained and uptight. It gives us permission to start a dialogue about what is bothering us and opens up channels of communication.

Try to give a few hugs per day to feel happier and more connected.

HAPPINESS IS A PERFUME YOU CANNOT
POUR ON OTHERS WITHOUT GETTING
A FEW DROPS ON YOURSELF.
— RALPH WALDO EMERSON

MINDSET MATTERS

Focus on your happiness today.
Don't wait for tomorrow.

Research has shown that mindfulness can improve immune function, as well as reduce muscle tension, headache, and other forms of chronic pain. It has longer-term impacts such as lowering blood pressure and cholesterol levels.

Mindfulness has also been shown to help with stress, anxiety, and depression.

Mindfulness is about appreciating what is happening today rather than worrying about what might happen in the future or agonizing over what happened in the past. It includes being curious and open to discovering new inspirations and information in the current setting.

You can be mindful by living in the present moment and appreciating what you have right now to be happy about. Take a few moments to observe your environment and notice things you haven't seen before. Instead of focusing on getting it done, try to enjoy doing it. When you sit down to a meal, don't just eat. Look at the colors, smell the aromas, think about all the tastes. If you are spending time with a friend or loved one, concentrate fully on them and what they are saying. Don't think about what you have to do next or what you are going to say. Listen deeply to what they are communicating and appreciate the time you are spending with them.

Mindset Matters is about creating positive emotions. Mindset Matters is like a tune-up for your car; you must do regular maintenance if you want it to run correctly. We need to set aside time and a means of routinely resetting our emotions to positive.

A PESSIMIST SEES THE DIFFICULTY
IN EVERY OPPORTUNITY.

AN OPTIMIST SEES THE OPPORTUNITY
IN EVERY DIFFICULTY.

– WINSTON CHURCHILL

PRACTICE THE 100/0 PRINCIPLE

This is how to guarantee your relationships will work.

"Positive Relationships" is one of the strongest concepts supported by the science of happiness. The more and better your relationships are, the happier you are. A foundational element to creating and improving positive relationships is a concept Al Ritter writes about in his book *The 100/0 Principle*.

Most of us go into a relationship believing that it should be a 50/50 exchange. Two people giving half each, which adds up to 100% – then we will all be happy. The challenge of 50/50 doesn't work a lot of the time. If one person is giving 50%, but the other person is only giving 30% because of some challenge they are experiencing in their lives, the relationship suffers.

Give 100% and expect nothing in return.

The other person can give 0%, but you will still be there for them because you want to give and you believe that relationship is important. If you have no expectation that they will call you, bring you flowers, remember your birthday, or behave in any particular way, you will not have a reason to be disappointed in them and they won't feel pressure to be someone different from who they are. Most likely, they will respond in kind, even though you are all right if they don't. They will appreciate your efforts and they will give more than 0%, and often more than 50% back to the relationship.

You will find abundance rather than scarcity in your relationship, so give 100% to the relationship and expect nothing in return.

THE ONLY WAY A RELATIONSHIP WILL LAST
IS IF YOU SEE YOUR RELATIONSHIP
AS A PLACE TO GIVE,
AND NOT A PLACE TO TAKE.
– ANTHONY ROBBINS

PRACTICE 100-LB ROCKS TO HELP PRIORITIZE YOUR DAY

Practicing the 100-pound Rocks part of being happy is feeling productive and believing we can make a difference each day. In order to make a difference, we need to make sure we complete tasks most related to accomplishing our goals. One method of prioritization is the "100-pound Rocks" rule.

Picture two rooms: One is filled with rocks and the other is empty. Every day, in order to reach our goals, we have to move as many rocks from the first room to the second room as we can. Each rock has a number on it from 1 to 100 that corresponds to the impact that particular rock will have on achieving our goals. If we can only move five rocks a day, we want to make sure they are the rocks that most help us reach our goals. For instance, if we move one 5-pound rock, three 15-pound rocks, and one 30-pound rock to the other room, at the end of the day we have moved five rocks and made 80 pounds of progress toward our goals (5 + 45 + 30 = 80).

The other option is to pick out five 100-pound rocks. This time, we have moved the same number of rocks, but made 500 pounds of progress toward our goals, making us over five times as productive. The fastest way to reach our goals is to take a few extra minutes to pick out the 100-pound rocks. Once the 100-pound rocks are gone, we will pick out the 99-pound rocks, and then the 98-pound rocks, etc. It is up to each person to define their 5-pound rocks and their 100-pound rocks. Ask, "Which will have the most impact on achieving my goals?"

However, some of the lower-value rocks may include reading non-essential email, answering texts or instant messages, playing games on our phone, surfing the web, Facebook, or your digital distraction of choice. Some high-value rocks include your relationships, your health, your career, that big project you have been procrastinating over, and anything else that will make a difference in someone else's life.

Write down a list of things you have to do today. Assign each item a size. Make sure your top three rocks are done first every day: *Find your 100-pound rocks and start making a difference that has impact.*

HAVE A PURPOSE
EVERY DAY

Stick to a new diet or exercise plan by connecting it to your Higher Purpose. Rather than exercising or dieting so you can look better, do it to help other people. Trying to look better is something we do for ourselves and it is not as motivational or inspiring as trying to do something for someone else. Connect your diet and exercise to a Higher Purpose and you will have more success. A healthy diet and exercise give us more energy, help us be more productive, and help us live longer. We might exercise or eat a healthy diet so that

- ★ we will be around long enough to help our children and grandchildren,
- ★ we can be around and healthy and when our friends need us,
- ★ our friends and family won't have to take care of us when we grow ill from a life of unhealthy habits,
- ★ we can bring more energy to work to help our peers and customers,
- ★ we can have more energy to help our favorite charity,
- ★ we can be more productive and advance our careers,
- ★ your own Higher Purpose.

How can you give to others by exercising and dieting? How can you be there for others by having more energy, being more productive, and living longer?

PRACTICE REGULAR SHORT-TERM WINS

Use a paper calendar to build habits. 92% of people are not successful in achieving their New Year's resolutions. That is because most people depend on willpower (which is a limited resource) rather than building new habits. Once something becomes a habit, you don't have to drain your willpower forcing yourself do it.

Pick something you want to change in order to be happier, like being on a diet, getting more organized, spending less money, or just finding ways to enjoy life. Schedule 15 minutes every day, preferably in the morning when your willpower is full, and spend that time working on your new habit. Plan your meals, make a list of two or three things you want to accomplish that day, work on your budget, or write down something fun you will make happen that day. Print out a paper calendar with 30 days on it. Every morning, when you complete your new habit-forming task, put an X on the calendar.

Keep the calendar in a prominent place where you can see it. Try to put an X on each day and not miss a day. If you miss a day, don't get discouraged. Just start over.

Keep working on your habit until you have 30 X's in a row. By that time, it should be habit, something you do automatically every day. Now you can start working on your next habit.

It is important not to get discouraged if you go through 2 or 3 calendars before you get 30 in a row. Just keep trying. Once you get the first habit, the others will come easier.

The brain thrives on short-term wins. Make them tough enough to be a challenge but not so tough that we realize we will never attain them. Knowing that a task is impossible will make you disengage.

IF YOU ARE GOING TO ACHIEVE
EXCELLENCE IN BIG THINGS,
YOU DEVELOP THE HABIT IN LITTLE MATTERS.
EXCELLENCE IS NOT AN EXCEPTION,
IT IS A PREVAILING ATTITUDE.
– COLIN POWELL

INCH-PEBBLES VS
MILE-STONES

Change old habits into happiness habits one tiny change at a time. If we want to increase our level of happiness, something has to change. Otherwise, we are staying in the same place and not growing. The best way to change is to create new habits or make adjustments to our old habits.

Changing habits is difficult even for the most disciplined people and changing lots of habits at once is almost impossible. The secret is to start small. Find one habit you can change a little bit and then focus on that until the change becomes part of your natural routine. For example if you want to exercise more, don't start by training for a marathon. Your willpower is limited and can easily get used up making yourself run long distances five times a week.

Instead, start your exercise by walking to your neighbor's house or half way down your block each day. Just a little walking each day will only take a few minutes and will take a minimal amount of willpower to complete. If you feel like walking further you can, but only put pressure on yourself to walk a little further. Once that has become part of your routine for 30 days or more, then you can extend the walk.

Often you will find you have extended your walks without even thinking about it. Later, you can add jogging for a small distance. The point is to start small and work up to it in small increments so it becomes a habit rather than something you dread doing. Look at it as attaining "inch-pebbles" as opposed to "mile-stones."

If you change and grow, you will be happier, especially if the change lasts. You can then move

on to other small changes so you are always
getting a little happier.

AIM FOR THE SKY, BUT MOVE SLOWLY,
ENJOYING EVERY STEP ALONG THE WAY.
IT IS ALL THOSE LITTLE STEPS
THAT MAKE THE JOURNEY COMPLETE.
– CHANDA KOCHHAR

FIND MEANING
IN WHAT YOU DO

Go make a difference
in someone's life.

One of the most common terms used in people's definitions of happiness is "meaning." We are all looking for meaning in our lives. One of the best ways to find meaning is to make a difference in someone else's life. Our challenge is we often measure the amount of meaning in our lives by the number of people who tell us we are making a difference.

Unfortunately, in people's busy lives they often don't take time or don't know how to stop and let someone know they made a difference. So we don't hear how important we are often enough and sometimes get discouraged.

Don't wait to hear that you matter from someone else. Don't measure your ability to make a difference by the number of people who find a way to share their feelings of gratitude. Instead, just start helping people. Find people to smile at or extend a helping hand. Make someone who seems down feel better. Donate your time to a charity. Help a friend with a move or navigate through an emotional challenge. Assist a colleague at work.

Find ways every day to make a difference for someone else, and you will be happier and live a more meaningful life.

MAN'S MAIN CONCERN IS NOT
TO GAIN PLEASURE OR TO AVOID PAIN
BUT RATHER TO SEE A MEANING IN HIS LIFE.
– VIKTOR FRANKL

KEEP A "HAPPINESS JAR"

Capturing memories of a great year helps make it a great year. Use a clear jar so you can see inside. Add movie tickets, wine corks, receipts from great meals you have had, and sticky notes with short summaries of a fun thing you did. Note whom you were with, what you did, and why it made you happy. Be creative: You will find all kinds of little reminders you can add.

Keep your Happiness Jar in a prominent place so you can look inside and relive many of your happy times and so you can be reminded to keep adding more happy memories. Just seeing the jar creates inspiration to do something that makes you happy. Share the happiness by letting visitors and friends add to your jar. It is exciting to watch what makes them happy. Decorate your jar and put the year on it. You can create a jar each year so you have years and years of happy memories you can revisit.

Giving makes you happier than keeping. Research has shown that giving money or something to a charity or to help someone else made people happier, and that happier people gave more money to help others, suggesting there is a virtue circle of giving and becoming happier, which leads to more giving. The research included giving people $5 or $20 and then assigning them a task of giving it away or spending it on themselves .Those people who gave the money to someone else were happier than were the people who spent it on themselves.

THE FOOLISH MAN SEEKS HAPPINESS
IN THE DISTANCE;
THE WISE MAN GROWS IT
UNDER HIS FEET.
– JAMES OPPENHEIM

PRACTICE GETTING IN THE FLOW

"Flow" is a state where you lose track of time and your surroundings. You are so caught up in what you are doing, your brain doesn't process unrelated outside information.

Mihaly Csikszentmihalyi, author of *Flow: The Psychology of Optimal Experience*, who is the leading expert on flow, found that people who became really absorbed in what they were doing had higher levels of happiness. The more they got into a flow, the happier they were.

Flow requires challenges that push us out of our comfort zone but are not too demanding. It requires that we know enough to do the task well while still enjoying learning and getting better. It is an optimal experience.

Find a project or activity where you are confident in your abilities but is still challenging for you. Turn off all distractions such as e-mail reminders, texts, instant messages, and other interruptions. Work for 45 minutes without interruption and see how much you can get done, then take 15 minutes to walk around and re-energize before you start again.

Don't work for 10 hours straight with 12 distractions per hour. You will leave feeling tired and with no sense of accomplishment You find Flow in 45-minute distraction-free intervals. You will be more productive and thus, happier.

THE SELF EXPANDS THROUGH
ACTS OF SELF-FORGETFULNESS.
— MIHALY CSIKSZENTMIHALYI

EXERCISE ON A REGULAR BASIS

Make time to exercise and you will be healthier, happier, and more productive. As it is, our time is constrained and we don't have enough of it to get everything done, but we should schedule time to exercise on a regular basis. Evidence from numerous researchers concludes there is a positive relationship between exercise and work-life balance.

People who take the time to exercise feel more self-efficacy. In other words they are confident they can get things done.

Completing a regular exercise routine gives them proof that they are capable of handling bigger challenges, including getting major projects at work done and making time for a happy home life.

Exercise also makes you happier. It gives you more energy. It also provides a mental and emotional break from your daily stress. It gives you time to think and process information. Research has shown that exercise was more effective than anti-depressant medication in reducing the symptoms of depression. Exercise improves your brain's ability to process information. Overall, exercise helps you think more clearly, feel more confident, and be more energetic, all of which helps you be better at your job.

MOVEMENT IS A MEDICINE FOR
CREATING CHANGE IN A PERSON'S
PHYSICAL, EMOTIONAL, AND MENTAL STATES.
– CAROL WELCH

SCHEDULE "ME-TIME"

We are busy with the craziness of life forcing us to move from one urgent matter to the next. School, work, kids, bills, and many other commitments absorb our time and willpower.

Instead of getting lost in the business of your life, schedule 15 minutes every morning where you are the priority. We can all find 15 minutes somewhere in our day. For 15 minutes, work on something that makes your life better. If you want to go on a diet, then spend that 15 minutes creating a menu for the day or preparing your meals. If you want to exercise more, spend that 15 minutes putting on some training shoes and walking. If you have a hobby you want to try, spend 15 minutes on the internet buying supplies or finding a quiet place to work each morning.

The key is to recognize that you and your goals are a priority. You deserve time to improve your life. It is best to start early before your energy and willpower gets sucked up by all of your other commitments. Once you have successfully found 15 minutes every day for a month or more, you can extend it to 30 minutes or an hour.

You are important. Prioritize time for yourself so you can connect happiness and success.

Change the social script to be more positive.

It is easy being average, but to be positive, you must often rewrite the social script. Sometimes, being positive means that people misunderstand your intentions, feel awkward, or make you feel awkward.

As leaders, we must have the courage to break and/or rewrite these scripts to increase adaptability and performance. We must help others get comfortable breaking social scripts that limit potential.

We must support and encourage positive outliers.

AS HUMANS, WE ACTUALLY REQUIRE
A SENSE OF MEANING TO THRIVE.
—ED DIENER

FINISH THE DAY
ON A POSITIVE NOTE

We can't remember every moment of every experience, so we selectively remember the highlights and the last few moments of them. We then categorize our memories based on those tidbits of the experience.

A really good experience that ends poorly will be categorized as bad while a bad experience that ends well will be categorized as good. One year from now, we will remember that in general, the experience was good or bad based on the highlight and our last memory. This is mostly an unconscious process, but we can influence it by purposely reviewing the good parts at conclusion of every experience.

Every night as you go to bed, think through the day and remember the good things that happened that day. A month from now, you will remember mostly good days and at the end of the year, you will believe you had a good year. Much of your happiness is based on your memories, and you can choose to focus on the bad memories and have a crummy life or focus on the good memories and have a great life.

Scanning for Positives

You can rewire (change) your brain intentionally to make it better at seeing the positive by devoting a good portion of your time and attention to identifying patterns, which will lead you to solutions. Once you have done it so long you see patterns and solutions, it becomes effortless to find the positives in your day. This is called the "Tetris Effect."

Meditate

Take a few minutes to clear the brain of its tendency to multi-task and create unnecessary and unhealthy stress. Research shows after just a few minutes of meditating, the brain was calmer and performed much better. Meditation gives the brain a rest

Become a doubler

Research has proven that by simply journaling about a positive experience the brain gets to relive it, thereby doubling the effect of the experience.

Write down all the positive things you experience before you end your day.

Practice the 20-Second Rule

Making small energy adjustments, we can reroute the path of least resistance and replace bad habits with good ones.

Happiness is a choice.

YOU DECIDE

ABOUT THE AUTHOR

DEVIN C. HUGHES is a highly
sought after motivational
speaker, author, and
mindfulness muse. He is the
author of eighteen books and
his approach draws from the
science of positive psychology,
positive organizational
research, appreciative inquiry,
neuroscience, mindset, and mindfulness.

Devin lives in San Diego, California, with his wife,
four daughters, and two rescue dogs.

www.devinchughes.com

Made in the USA
Monee, IL
25 October 2020